Acknowledgement

All copyrighted works in this collection are produced under license with
print permission granted by the following publishers.

Acknowledged with special thanks to :

Schott Music Limited
Universal Music Publishing Editio Musica Budapest
Faber Music Limited
Forsyth Brothers Limited
The Associated Board of the Royal Schools of Music
Breitkoft & Härtel, Wiesbaden
Polskie Wydawnictwo Muzyczne—PWM Edition
Universal Edition A.G.
Chester Music Limited —Music Sales Group

TEACHERS' CHOICE, SELECTED PIANO REPERTORY

(contains ABRSM examination pieces of the 2015 & 2016 syllabus)

Edited and annotated by Josephine Koh

CONTENTS

Studies & Exercises

Grade 3

Pieces

Studies

Editor's Preface

This compilation is drawn from authentic sources, with suggested editorial suggestions for teaching and learning purposes. I would recommend that teachers assist students to find for themselves, the best approaches to meet their physical and musical abilities.

Pedagogical points are provided on what constitutes acceptable performance practice, which would include articulation, pedaling and tempo. As musical understanding and stylistic practices evolve with time, the approach in this collection serves to meet students' needs while preparing for the ABRSM examinations. Musical perspectives concerning tone, sound, articulation, and dynamics may vary in different cultural and social contexts. With various sensibilities highlighted in the explanatory notes, teachers may find it helpful when facilitating their students' imagination and technique. When in doubt, I would highly recommend that original or Urtext scores be consulted.

Fingering

They are suggestive and in no way to be conformed. Good fingering is important. Decide on what works best based on:

      (i)   efficient facilitation of fingers that would help establish fluency in the playing.

      (ii)   the natural weight of each finger that would project a good sound and tone quality.

      (iii)   good, relaxed muscular control on the whole; over the hands, fingers and joints

Metronome markings

Most are suggested speeds to suit the mood and character of the pieces.

Articulation

Most baroque and classical works contain editorial suggestions which reflect the stylistic practices of the periods. These articulations, however, are often varied by different performers.

Dynamics and performance directions

Additional editorial suggestions are indicated in brackets or below the scores.

Pedal Marks

Pedaling has been indicated in detail in most instances. Harmony plays a determinant role in making decisions on pedal changes. Special effects, stylistic features and other considerations based on the mood of a piece may require the use of the pedal in an unconventional manner. At higher grades, pedaling technique often becomes more demanding, which often contribute to the overall effect of a piece. In most cases, a musical performance requires good footwork and a sensitive ear to achieve the intended effects.

Josephine Koh

Editorial Symbols

The editorial symbols used throughout this series are explained below.

Slurred notes, to be played *smoothly*.
They are usually found in original scores and sources.

Dotted slurs are editorial marks which suggest that the notes are to be played *smoothly in one musical direction.*

Long dotted lines indicate suggested *phrasing,* usually 2, 4 or 8 bars.

This mark is used to indicate a *point of breath,* more significant than the end of a phrase.

The note is be held to its *full value* but *separated* from the next. This creates a non-legato effect.

(3 1 2 4)   An *alternative* set of fingering suggested.

Pedal mark suggests the movement of the foot.

This suggests the use of *non-legato pedaling.*

This suggests the use of *legato pedaling.* The pedal change is made after the next note is sounded.

The dynamic marking is editorial, i.e. not notated in the original sources.

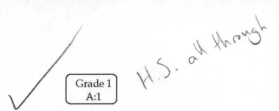

Arietta
Lesson Five from Op. 42

Clementi

An arietta is a short song. This simple piano piece with a tuneful melody in C major is a delightful piece for the young student. A graceful, legato touch with slurred notes is essential to bring out the elegant style of this classical work. It is important to ensure that both hands are well coordinated on the beats, without the left hand being too loud. Each phrase is 4-bars in length, with articulation marks and fingering being editorial. Slight arm pressure can be applied to bring out the shape of the melody and phrasing.

Menuett in G
from Notebook for Nannerl

L. Mozart

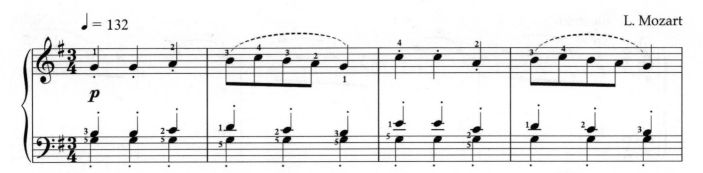

(play the left hand semi-detached throughout)

A simple and lively dance in 3/4 time, this piece offers some interesting challenges for the Grade 1 student. The opening chords have to co-ordinate well with the melody, achieving a good sense of balance of tone in both hands. Quavers would contrast with a legato touch. As they move up the higher register (bars 5-7 and 11-13) the melodic shape and direction have to be clearly shown. It is recommended that the left hand plays detached throughout, being quieter than the right hand, and keeping the crotchet beats even and in time.

Allegretto in C

Neefe

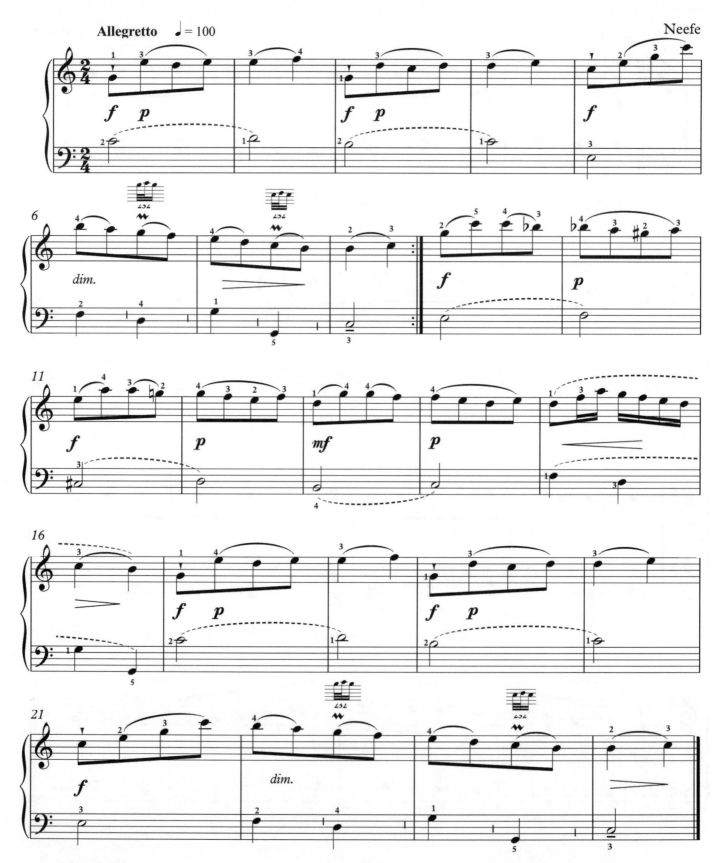

A melodious and charming work, this song-like piece is well written for the young pianist. The beauty lies in the regular phrasing, simple rhythms and elegant melody in the right hand. Dynamic contrasts of *f* and *p* and the descending sequences from bars 9-14 provide further interests. It is important for students to maintain a consistent pulse with evenly played quavers and semiquavers. Phrases need to be well shaped, with varied articulation and clean finger work to ensure that the ornaments are distinct. Slurs, articulation, metronome marks and fingering are editorial.

3

Heiteres Lied
Op. 36

A. Gedicke

Andantino ♩ = 72 - 76

This cheerful folk song takes on a 2/4 skipping meter. Other than a few accidentals, the C major melody has distinct staccato notes and semiquavers that require good legato finger work. The left hand supports with perfect 5ths in the opening bars, which resemble bagpipes. The phrases are regular, of which repetitive rhythms are kept within the strict meter. Changes of dynamics provide interest, with the left hand sounding mainly on the off beats.

Waltz
No. 5 from 22 Little Piano Pieces

Lajos Papp

This waltz has a modal quality. The melody which begins in the bass is first accompanied by lightly detached harmonies in the right hand. The touch has to be weighted for the left hand (bars 1–12) and smoothly played, like a cello line which leans towards the end of each 2-bar phrase. At bar 13, with the melody shifted to the right hand, it becomes more prominent. The mood brightens, with louder dynamics which gradually softens and slows down towards the end.

My, What a din the Cuckoos are making!

Leo Ornstein

The opening notes portrays the sounds of 2 cuckoo birds. A clear and crisp staccato touch would be apt to project the effect. Smooth flowing quavers provide contrast and at a much softer dynamic level. Bars 9 – 16, would be somewhat challenging for the student, as the passage takes off very softly, gradually gets louder and faster, with one cuckoo chasing the other, before landing on a chord at bar 16. Set in the key of A minor, the final 8 bars repeat the opening 8 bars.

6

Five Finger Position
Op. 82, No. 1

Moderato

Gurlitt

Slurs and Ornaments

Adapted by Josephine Koh

The study by Gurlitt focuses on strengthening the five fingers in the C position.

The study on slurs and ornaments would help students to achieve the effects of the ornaments required for Neefe's Allegretto in C on page 3

Staccato Chords

Adapted by Josephine Koh

♩ = 100 - 132

3.

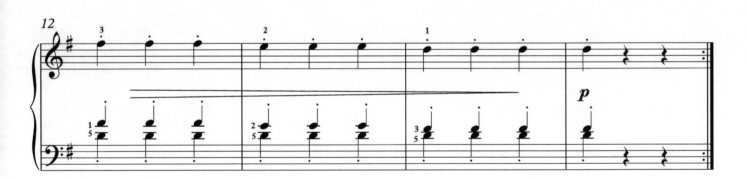

This study is adapted and developed from L.Mozart's Menuett in G on page 2. The study of these chords would ensure that the notes are well co-ordinated between both hands and the precision of the touch for the staccatos is achieved. Played with firm and curved fingers, the student would see fingers being strenthened from this exercise.

Blank Page

Impertinence
HWV 494

Allegro ♩ = 84

Handel

This Baroque piece has a rather interesting 'impertinent' (unruly, impolite) character portrayed by the imitative melodic phrases, and exchanges between the right and the let hand. The simple 2-part counterpoint reveals rising and falling pitch patterns, of which varied dynamics are suggested here. A detached touch can be stylistically applied to the crotchets, with non-legato minims giving the piece its 'impertinent', steadfast effect. Slurred quavers are recommended to provide contrast for this lively, dance-like piece.

A Trumpet Minuet

marcato
(play the notes marked and separated)

A bass melody opens the piece, which resembles a bassoon or a very resonant cello. The trumpet melody enters at bar 9, in the baroque clarino style with its high melodic range. It has a bright, confident character which makes use of accented notes, detached and slurred articulation. A 3-part texture emerges at the same time, of which the inner notes of the left hand should be played softer than the first bass note. The piece is appealing, of which good balance and co-ordination have to be achieved between both hands. It is important to keep to a prominent metric pulse.

11

Allegro in D

Leopold Mozart

(legato in the both hands)

A lyrical piece in ternary form (A: bars 1-8, B: bars 9-16, C: bar 17-24), one can imagine this work being composed by the father of Wolfgang Mozart for his children. The phrases are regular and well balanced, to be played with a legato touch that gives slight emphasis to mark out the main beats; yet without bringing about undue accents. The left hand, would ascend steadily, in counterpoint with the melody before tapering downwards at the end of each phrase. All quavers are expected to flow evenly. Additional dynamics and phrase marks have been added for a musical rendition of the piece.

Hot Rolls

No. 8 from *The Windmill*

Fly

This piece has a leisurely, peaceful and scenic appeal. It conjures a countryside landscape, of which rolls of hay are being dried under the sun. The melody is simple, consisting of short phrases which occasionally moves to the left hand. Varied dynamics would effectively portray the character of the piece, with the climax at bar 22. Pedalling (optional) has been suggested to enrich the effect. All detached notes should not be played too crisp or short.

14

Raindrops

No. 5 from *Splash!*

M. Lysenko

'Raindrops' are presented characteristically with lightly detached notes, repeated notes and some quick flow of semiquavers. The left hand accompaniment on the off beats give the piece its playful effect. Composed by the Ukrainian composer Mykola Lysenko, the melody has an interesting folk flavour. At bar 13, the melody shifts to the left hand before developing a sense of drama in the last few bars that closes the piece with a change in tempo, a pause and the sudden downpour that ends with a big splash!

15

The Little Flower

Die kleine Blume / Une petite fleur

N. Podgornov

Affettuoso ♩ = 69

This piece takes on a graceful simplicity, marked by the legato lines and calm harmonies in the left hand. A well controlled touch, with application of arm weight would project a nice and warm tone suited to the character of the piece. The rise and fall of the quavers, with dynamics indicated, calls for an approach that is sensitive to the description of the little flower - small, delicate and pretty. The left hand chords should never overwhelm the melody at any point. Some flexibility of the tempo, not being restricted by a metric pulse would be appropriate.

Lazy River
from *Get it Together!*

Carol Barratt

Dreamily- very slow

As the title suggests, this piece takes on a lazy, meandering mood with its melody derived from a pentatonic scale. The phrases are repetitive, with changes in the left hand harmonies and accompaniment. The 6/8 time signature with the repeated left hand chords give a gentle swing to the piece. With a legato touch within the slow tempo, the effect of the piece can be hypnotic. Though the dynamics are mainly soft, some undulating nuances with a slight lilt to the phrases would express the piece effectively. Pedal marks are as indicated in the original score.

17

Twisters

from *Miniatures for Piano, Op. 5*

Garścia

This piece begins with a characteristic twisting effect, with the oscillating double notes in the left hand. The melody, in contrast, is a simple 4-bar folk-like tune which repeats 3 times. It is important to ensure that all quavers and semiquavers are played evenly, particularly with gradual changes in the dynamics. Bars 12 to 18 transfers the twisting figure to the right hand. Further changes in colour can be dramatized with expressive accents in the left hand and slight slowing down at bar 17. The quiet ending too brings on a special rhythmic effect. Refer to page 20 for supportive exercise.

Legato Melody and Staccato Chords
Op.82 No.34

Gurlitt

Allegro

1.

Legato Melody with Shape

Moderato ♩ = 120

Josephine Koh

2.

Double Notes for the Left Hand
Exercise for 'Twisters'

3.

Allegro
1st movement from Sonatina in C, Op. 36 No.1

Muzio Clementi

This delightful sonatina movement has been a most appealing work for generations of young pianists. The C major melody is bright and cheerful, with scalic movement that has to be played evenly and with a good sense of musical direction. Clementi's classical style is revealed in the homophonic texture, with a light accompaniment that consists of alberti bass figures. The phrasing is regular, best to be performed with varied articulation and dynamics. Additional slurs, articulation, dynamics and fingering are editorial, suited to the modern day student.

Allegro in C,
Wq 116/53

C.P.E. Bach

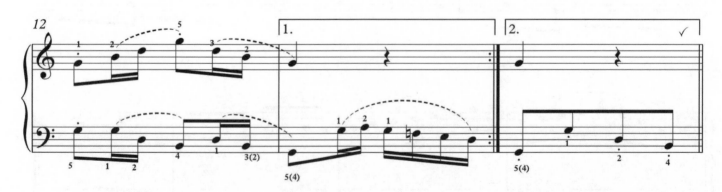

C.P. E. Bach's pre-classical piece is indeed approachable for the Grade 3 student. Composed for 2-parts, the left hand alternates between playing harmony notes and providing simple counterpoint. By employing a mix of detached and slurred notes, the dance-like character of the piece would emerge. The grace notes should never be rushed, but lean elegantly onto the start of each group of semiquavers.

Technically, it is important to work with well curved fingers. A firm touch, along with clear articulation would serve the piece well, particularly the light trills. Detached notes must not be too dry and crisp. The dynamics and fingering are editorial.

Allegretto in E flat

No. 6 from *Différentes petites pièces faciles et agréables*

Haydn

This is an interesting, yet challenging work for the Grade 3 student. The E flat major key resonates with a rich tone when played with a confident and firm touch at the beginning. The cadences and phrases are clear, with detached notes of bar 10 giving gusto to the piece. The continuous flow of semiquavers from bars 14 to 25, followed by slurred couplets are challenging passages.

It is important to sort out the fingering of the right hand on its own at a slow tempo before taking off at a faster pace. Changes in dynamics or subtle nuances applied to the undulating melodic line would be appropriate. Repeated notes of bars 29 to 31 have to be kept light. The final 4 bars form an effective conclusion for the piece.

Vivace
4th movt from Sonatina in A minor, Op. 136, No. 4

Vivace ♩ = 96

Reinecke

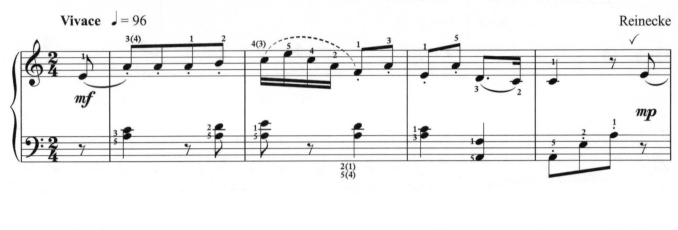

This piece is written in a typical classical style with balanced 4-bar phrases within a homophonic texture. The opening melody with its repeated notes becomes the primary motif of the piece. Although composed in the minor key, the quick semiquavers, detached notes, dotted rhythms and leaps give the melody at lively character. Clear finger articulation is important; and likewise the need to maintain a consistent rhythmic pulse throughout, except for bar 18. Co-ordination between both hands has to be assured, with careful attention given to the slurs, detached notes and dynamic changes.

Bars 26 to 30 provide a moment of stylistic contrast to the main theme. The descending sequences that follow gradually soften the music. An element of surprise is brought about by the final 2 bars that end with a positive and loud A major chord.

Schulstunde (School Lesson)
Op. 36, No. 2

Allegro moderato ♩ = 96

Gedicke

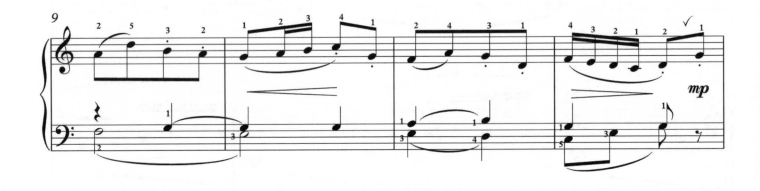

This piece begins in good cheer. With a lively 2/4 meter, the slurred and detached notes give a skipping character to the melody in C major. The regular phrases have been marked, with edited dynamics to provide interest and contrast. Held notes in the left hand of bars 9 to 16 result in a 3-part texture - a change from the chordal accompaniment of bars 1-8. A more assertive section in A minor from bar 17 brings the piece to its climax at bars 21-24. The opening melody returns at bar 25, somewhat quieter, before ending the piece with a definitive perfect cadence.

Blank Page

Melancholy

from *Little Stories in Jazz*

Mike Schoenmedhl

The melody and harmonies of this piece are reminiscent of blues, with the chromatic notes, held notes in the bass and quieter inner parts. The result is a sentimental feeling, with the generally low range of notes and slow rhythms. A lighter moment emerges from bars 9 to 12, before the rich texture returns again. Use of the pedal is recommended, to enhance the effect of the swing on the main beats. A controlled mellow tone, played with slight pressure from the arms would project the mood of the piece effectively.

Foxtrot II

from *Leichte Tänze*

Seiber

The character of the foxtrot is established by the leaping bass accompaniment with the signature ♪ ♩. rhythm in the melody. With the catchy tune of the right hand and the left hand keeping to its constant beat throughout, this piece is simply fun to learn and play. The rhythmic style of this dance is best brought out with a non legato touch in both hands.

It is important to ensure that the touch is never too heavy, of which the chords need to attain a light bouncy effect. It would be effective to practise with hands separately, particularly to work out the various syncopated effects of the right hand, before putting both hands together. As no dynamics are provided in the original score, additional fingering, slurs and dynamics are editorial.

a Maribel
Aurora

Jesús Torres

In all quietness, Aurora means 'sunrise', a calm and tranquil piece composed in a modern idiom. The harmonies are unusual, which attempt to create the magical atmosphere at twilight, cleverly evoked by the effect of the sustaining pedal. With gentle moving quavers, a sparse texture, gradual changes of dynamics, syncopations (bars 7-8) and distant tones, this is an imaginative piece that presents a new sound world.

Finger Articulation

Technical Study
Grade 3

Allegro ♩ = 108 - 120

Czerny

Practice Exercises for Foxtrot

Adapted from C:5 on pages 31-32 by Seiber

Exercise (a) : Repeat the passage, keeping the left hand constant.

Exercise (b) : Repeat the passage, paying attention to the rhythm of the melody.

Exercise (c). Play this melody, accompanied by the same chords as in Exercise (b)

Lilting Effect of Slurs
Op. 139, No. 41

Czerny

Technical Study Grade 3

Allegro molto ♩ = 120

Scales and Arpeggios for Piano (Grades 1 to 8)
J Koh's Fingering Method

Students can now learn scales and arpeggios in the most enjoyable and effective way. *J Koh's Fingering Method* develops the learners' cognitive skills by using a combination of visual, auditory and tactile systems. Now available in print, this proven method used for training gifted children is specially produced to assist students prepare for the ABRSM graded piano practical examinations. Success assured! The series from Grades 1 to 5 focuses on establishing good fingering habits. The *Fingering & Tonality Method* for Grades 6 to 8 continues the development of technical competence in piano students based on key and chord structures.

Practice in Music Theory (Grades 1 to 8)
Revised Edition
by Josephine Koh

The revised edition of the *Practice in Music Theory* series is a set of highly recommended instructional workbooks for students who wish obtain a sound foundation in music theory. The *J Koh's* teaching approach is academic and logical, yet musically conceived. Progressive topics are set out to guide students through their understanding of the fundamental musical concepts and ideas. Based on the requirements of the ABRSM theory syllabus, this series has :

- clear teaching points and graphical illustrations
- explanatory notes that are applied throughout the series
- exercises of progressive difficulty that provide students with sufficient practice to master the topics and concepts learnt
- updated information and study notes that are most effective for reference and revision.

Rhythmatics
by Josephine Koh & Florence Koh

Group notes, write beats, identify time signatures and complete bars with missing notes or rests — all these tasks with **Rhythmatics**, the most sought after musical learning aid for young children. Attractive colour cards, each with a particular colour and shape corresponds to a specific time value. With the cards to be arranged on the base whiteboard mathematically, the child visualises the concept instantaneously and is able to perceive the number of beats in a bar. Most suitable for children between ages of 4 to 9, **Rhythmatics** is recommended for the study of music theory up to Grade 2.

Teachers' Choice, Selected Piano Repertory & Studies for Grades 1,2 &3 is compiled to provide teachers and students with good options for the 2015 & 2016 ABRSM piano examinations.

* This collection of interesting and appealing piano pieces contains editorial suggestions for pedagogical purposes. Most teachers will find the performance points helpful in developing stylistic awareness in the students.

* Examination requirements aside, details on articulation, dynamics, fingering, pedal marks and tempo serve to provide a directed approach for students to strive towards achieving musical excellence and perfection.

* Effective technical studies suited to each level have been carefully selected, forming in themselves, supplementary materials to enhance technical competence.

* Most important of all, enjoy the high standards of music typography - such clear, professionally laid scores supported by modern publishing technology and musical semiotics. The digital print on quality cream-coloured paper ensures comfort in the reading of music scores.

Josephine Koh
BA(EM), FTCL, ARCM, L(Mus)TCL, LTCL
Bösendorfer Artiste, Conductor, Theorist & Author

Josephine Koh is a concert pianist, resident author and managing director of Wells Music Publishers. Professionally, she is the principal of Josephine Koh Music Studio. A conductor and music director at the Centre for the Arts, National University of Singapore, Ms Koh has been appointed as artiste for Bösendorfer Pianos of Vienna, Austria since 2009.

Other published titles include:
Practice in Music Theory Grades 1-8
Practice in Music Theory for the Little Ones, Books A and B
Rhythmatics
Quick Study for Piano Diploma Students
Scales and Arpeggios for Piano, Fingering Method, Grades 1-8
Teachers' Choice, Selected Piano Repertory, Grades 1-8
Musical Forms and Terms
Understanding Orchestration, The Orchestra and its Instruments

Wells Music Publishers

ISBN 981092408-9

9 789810 924089

WMP 2215